EXPLORING
HOUSES and HOMES

Cliff Lines

Illustrated by Stephen Wheele

Exploring the Past

Exploring Buildings

Exploring Castles

Exploring Clothes

Exploring Communications

Exploring Farming

Exploring Houses and Homes

Exploring Industry

Exploring People

Exploring Schools

Exploring Shopping

Exploring Sport and Recreation

Exploring Transport

Series editor: Stephen Setford
Designed by: Marilyn Clay

Cover picture: At home in the 1950s

First published in 1989 by
Wayland (Publishers) Ltd
61 Western Road, Hove
East Sussex, England BN3 1JD

© Copyright 1989 Wayland (Publishers) Ltd

British Library Cataloguing in Publication Data

Lines, C.J. (Clifford John), *1926–*
    Exploring houses and homes.
    1. Great Britain. Social life, history
    I. Title   II. Series
    941

    ISBN 1–85210–679–4

Phototypeset by Kalligraphics Ltd, Horley, Surrey
Printed in Italy by G. Canale C.S.p.A., Turin
Bound in the UK by The Bath Press, Avon

Contents

1 Introduction

What kind of house do you live in? Is it a bungalow, a flat, a terraced house or a country cottage? Whatever the shape and size of your home, like most others it will have a number of rooms with furniture, heating and lighting to make them comfortable. We take all these things for granted, but if we could go back in a time capsule we would find that homes in the past were different and had fewer comforts. It is difficult to imagine that there was a time when glass was too expensive to use in windows and floors were covered with straw.

An unusual home for a family: a converted Second World War (1939–45) motor torpedo boat.

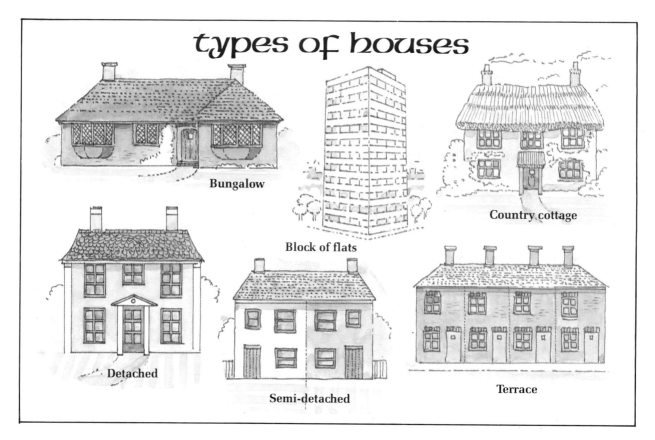

types of houses

Bungalow

Block of flats

Country cottage

Detached

Semi-detached

Terrace

There are lots of activities in this book which will help you to discover what homes were like in your district in the past. There are also ideas for projects which you and your friends can take part in. Find out how old your home is: it may be much older than you think.

Above are examples of some of the different types of homes.

Projects to do:

● Make a chart of the different kinds of home the members of your class live in.

● Make a photographic record of the different types of home in your area. Which is the most common type? Is there a reason for this?

● Make a study of another part of your town or city. Are the types of homes there similar to the ones in your own area?

The modern home

Only a few people live in a brand-new house. Most of us live in homes which were built some

A row of old, terraced houses being converted into flats.

time in the past and which have been altered over the years. Alterations are usually made to make the home more up to date and comfortable to live in. Most of the houses built in the 1950s did not have a garage because few people owned cars. If there is space, these houses are likely to have had garages added or a parking space made, because the majority of families now own a car.

There have been many changes in kitchens in recent years, too. New labour-saving equipment, such as washing-machines and dishwashers, have made housework easier. Kitchens have also become easier places in which to work, with fitted cupboards, sink units, and special work surfaces.

There have also been many recent improvements to make homes warmer and better lit. One of the biggest changes has been the installation of central heating. This allows all rooms to be kept warm, instead of only those where there is a fire. Double glazing and other ways of saving energy have helped to keep out draughts and reduce heating costs.

Many changes are now being made to homes by the people who live in them by using DIY (short for 'do it yourself') fittings and equipment. Ask your parents to help you make a list, like the one below, of the changes which they have made to your home. Why were these changes made?

One of the ground-floor rooms of this house has been altered into a garage for the family's car.

Changes to my home	Year	Reason
Fitted kitchen	1988	Modernize kitchen
Repainted lounge	1987	Make it brighter
Patio	1985	For barbecues!
Insulated loft	1983	Cut down on heating bills

Before and after the 1939–45 war

When your parents were young, homes were not as easy to run or as comfortable as they are today. During the 1950s and 1960s, some of the things we take for granted were just coming on to the market and many people could not afford to buy them. Newly married couples had to save up to buy their first washing-machine and refrigerator. Only wealthy people had freezers and dish-washers. New houses and flats were built with central-heating systems, while older homes still used coal fires, although boilers and radiators were beginning to be installed.

Many homes were cold and draughty, with no double glazing or insulation to keep the heat in.

Before the 1939–45 war, when your grand-parents were young, people's homes were less

A kitchen in a home in the mid-1930s from The Illustrated London News *of 1936. At the time, this kitchen was considered very 'modern'.*

A mother and her children in the lounge of their home in the early 1960s.

comfortable than they are today. There was a coal fire in the living-room, but other rooms were not heated. Some people had electric or gas cookers, but many cooked their food in ovens heated by coal fires. In the living-room, there was usually a 'wireless' (radio) and a 'gramophone' for playing records. Television sets were very expensive and most people went out to the cinema for entertainment. Rich people kept servants to do the housework, cooking and washing. Poorer people had to do these tasks by hand, without the help of the machines we use today.

Make a chart like the one below and ask your parents and grandparents to help you fill in the columns for the 1930s and 1960s.

Homes in the 1930s and 1960s	
1930s	1960s
No TVs	Black-and-White TVs
Coal fires	Some central heating
No refrigerators	Many refrigerators
No machines	Many machines

A home in 1910

Many people live in houses which were built between about 1880 and 1914. At that time British cities were growing rapidly and rows of terraced houses were built to provide people with homes. The terraced houses were long and narrow, with a garden at the back.

The front room, called the parlour, had a fireplace and gas lighting. It was seldom used, except when visitors came or there was a special occasion, such as a wedding. The family used the living-room, which also had a fireplace and a view to the back garden.

In the kitchen, there was a pantry and a large

This is the ground-floor plan of a house built around the end of the last century.

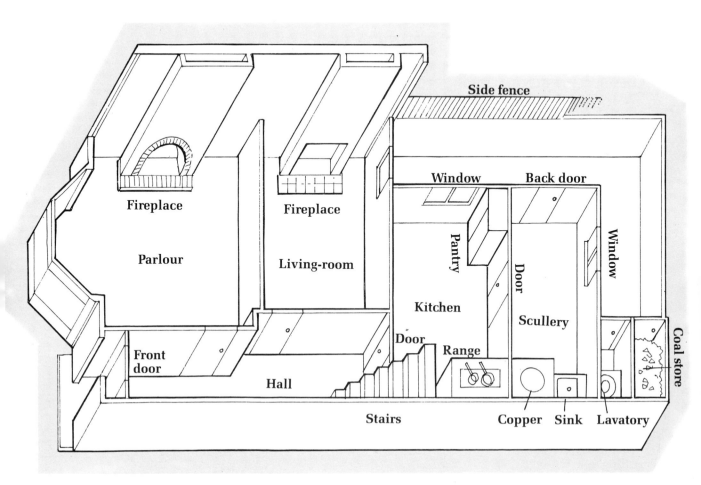

iron range, heated by a coal fire. The scullery, a small room off the kitchen, had a sink with a cold water tap above it and a 'copper' alongside. Water was heated in the copper by a fire underneath it. The copper was usually used for washing clothes.

Upstairs, the largest bedrooms had fireplaces, but were lit by candles or oil lamps. They contained a wash-stand with a marble top and a mirror. On the wash-stand stood a china bowl, which was filled with water from a jug and used for washing. There was no bathroom and baths were taken in the kitchen in a metal bath filled with hot water from the copper.

Many improvements have been made to these houses since they were built, but they still contain evidence of how they were once used. Look for clues in a house of this period with the help of the chart opposite.

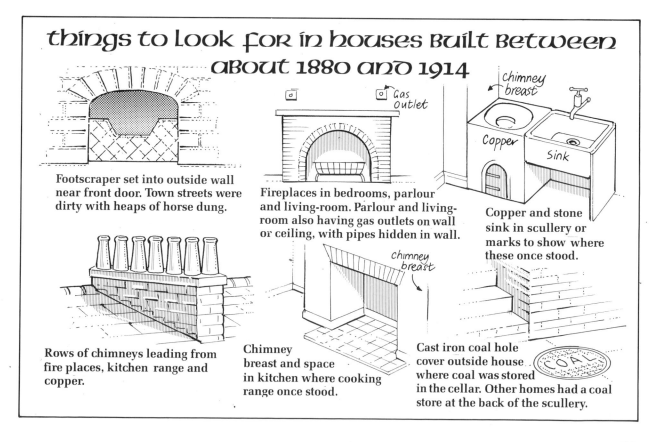

things to look for in houses built between about 1880 and 1914

Footscraper set into outside wall near front door. Town streets were dirty with heaps of horse dung.

Fireplaces in bedrooms, parlour and living-room. Parlour and living-room also having gas outlets on wall or ceiling, with pipes hidden in wall.

Gas Outlet

chimney breast

Copper

Sink

Copper and stone sink in scullery or marks to show where these once stood.

Rows of chimneys leading from fire places, kitchen range and copper.

chimney breast

Chimney breast and space in kitchen where cooking range once stood.

Cast iron coal hole cover outside house where coal was stored in the cellar. Other homes had a coal store at the back of the scullery.

COAL

3 | Victorian times

Upstairs-downstairs

Two groups of people lived in the homes of rich Victorians. There was the owner and his family, who lived in the main part of the house, and the servants. The servants slept in small attic rooms under the roof and lived in the servants' quarters, which were often in the basement. Wealthy families could afford several servants. There was a cook, a butler, a nursemaid to look after the children and one or two more maids.

The lives of the members of the family and the servants were kept as separate as possible. The servants stayed out of sight and cleaned and tidied the main rooms when the family was not present. Young girls, who worked as maids, were called 'tweenies' because their work took them *between* the upstairs rooms used by the family and the kitchen and servants' rooms in the basement of the house.

The family liked to entertain friends at home with musical evenings and parties. These took place in the drawing-room, with meals being eaten in the dining-room nearby. The children spent most of their time in the nursery at the top of the house.

The Victorians liked to fill their rooms with elaborate furniture, and decorate their chairs, tables and mantelpieces with needlework and lace. The servants had a great deal to do because there were no labour-saving devices. The diary opposite shows how a 'tweenie' spent her day. Make a similar diary for a young person you know who is at work.

A 'tweenie' had many unpleasant jobs to do in a Victorian household, such as getting coal for the fires. This picture is a Victorian advertisement for Richmond gas fires.

"WHY DON'T THEY GET A RICHMOND GAS FIRE?"

This picture from The Graphic *of 1893 shows afternoon tea being taken in the house of a wealthy Victorian family.*

A tweenie's day	
6.00 a.m.	Get up. Draw blinds. Make early morning tea and wake other servants
7.00	Clean fireplaces; set and light fires. Clean front step, stairs and landings. Polish door brasses. Collect hot-water jugs to take to bedrooms.
8.30	Serve dining-room breakfasts. Breakfast in kitchen afterwards. Help with washing-up.
9.00	Clean dining-room. Start morning's housework. Make beds.
12.30 p.m.	Serve lunch in dining-room. Lunch in kitchen afterwards.
1.30	Clear dining-room. Help with washing-up.
2.00–3.30	Free time.
3.30–5.00	Answer door to visitors. Serve tea.
5.00–7.00	Clean silver and check fires.
7.00	Serve at dinner.
7.30	Prepare bedrooms.
8.00	Serve coffee.
8.30	Supper in kitchen.
9.30	Check downstairs fires are safe for night. Help with washing up.
11.00	Go to bed.

Homes in the industrial towns

During the nineteenth century, factories sprang up on the coalfields of the Midlands and the North. They used machines, driven by steam power, which could produce goods in large quantities to sell in Britain and other parts of the world. People left the countryside in large numbers to work in these factories and houses were put up quickly and cheaply in terraces, which were

a Back~to~Back home of 1830

Stairs to floor below

Fireplace

Stairs to room above

Door to shared hallway

Cooking range

Simple wooden furniture

A drawing of a typical back-to-back home of the nineteenth century.

A row of terraced houses in Manchester. They were built for factory workers who came to the city from the countryside in the 1850s.

crowded together near the factories.

A home for a family in Birmingham consisted of two rooms in a terraced house which, to keep the cost low, was built back-to-back with another, so that three of the four walls were shared with neighbours. There was no garden or proper kitchen and candles were used for lighting. Water came from a pump in a courtyard, where there were also earth lavatories and a wash-house shared with other families. The country cottages these people had left had no better facilities; but in the towns thousands of families were crowded together, allowing disease to spread very easily. Today, many of these houses have been pulled down, but some have been improved and people still live in them.

Some employers, like Robert Owen at New Lanark in Scotland, and the Strutts at Belper in Derbyshire, built better-quality houses for their workers. At Belper, the cotton workers' homes had a living-room and a scullery on the ground floor, and two bedrooms above them.

Draw a front view of your home and compare it with the one opposite.

A farm cottage in the 1850s

Until 1850, more people in Britain lived in the countryside than in towns. Most were farm workers and their homes can still be seen in many parts of Britain. They lived in small cottages which had a roof covered in thatch or stone tiles. The floors were made of stone slabs, bricks or hard-packed earth. The most important room in

A painting of the inside of a farmworker's cottage in the first half of the nineteenth century.

the house was the kitchen, which was often the living-room too, because the fire used for cooking kept it warm. A door in the kitchen led into the pantry, where there was a tub which held water from a well in the garden.

The kitchen ceiling was low and supported by thick wooden beams, along which hams, onions and dried herbs were hung. The kitchen furniture was very simple: a wooden table, stools to sit on and a dresser for storing plates, cutlery and the few things the family owned. There was very little furniture in the rest of the house. In Scotland and parts of Wales, the beds, called box beds, were out of sight in cupboards or behind curtains. Sometimes there was a bedroom under the roof, which was usually reached by a ladder.

The lavatory, or privy as it was called, was a wooden hut near the back door, in which there was a bucket under a wooden seat. The sewage was thrown into a ditch or dug into the garden.

Draw a plan of one floor of your home using the same scale as the plan below of a shepherd's cottage. Is the area of your floor bigger or smaller than the shepherd's?

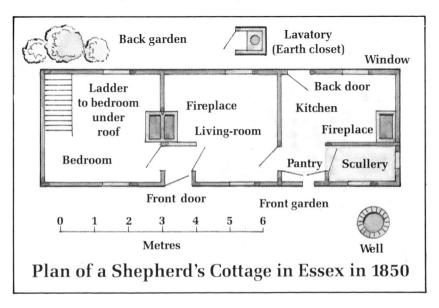

Plan of a Shepherd's Cottage in Essex in 1850

4 From 1500 to 1800

Homes as workplaces

Until the Industrial Revolution in the nineteenth century, craftsmen worked in their homes or in a workshop behind the house. A shoemaker in the sixteenth century, for example, used the front room of his home as a workshop. Shoes were sold to customers through the open front of the workshop, which was closed at night by shutters. There was a kitchen on the ground floor and rooms for the shoemaker and his family above. Under the roof lived the apprentices who were learning the trade.

Weavers and stocking knitters in the silk and woollen industries also worked at home. Their

The interior of a weaver's cottage in Scotland towards the end of the 1700s. The weaver is at work on his loom (left-hand side).

A street of old weavers' houses in the Bethnal Green area of London. Note the large windows on the top floor to let in as much light as possible.

looms were often placed in rooms at the top of the house. These rooms had long windows to catch as much light as possible, which help us today to identify weavers' houses. Scottish weavers often lived in single-storey cottages with the weaving shop at one end of the building.

Other tradesmen had jobs which required them to live close to their workplace. For the miller, his wind- or watermill was often his home because he had to be prepared to get up in the night. In the eighteenth and nineteenth centuries, toll houses on the turnpike roads and lock-keepers' cottages on the canals were specially designed so that the keeper could see approaching traffic.

Draw or paint a scene of the outside or inside of a craftsman's home.

An Elizabethan timber-framed home

Have you ever been inside a timber-framed home, such as Anne Hathaway's cottage near Stratford-upon-Avon? In parts of the country where building stone was scarce, Elizabethan houses were

Speke Hall, Liverpool, is an impressive example of Elizabethan architecture.

built with a wooden frame. The frame was made of oak and the spaces between the beams were filled with hazel or willow branches woven together and then covered with plaster. Glass could only be made in small pieces, so it was set into strips of lead and mounted in an iron window-frame. Stone floors made the rooms cold and warmth was provided by large fireplaces which burned logs, or coal in some districts. The only form of lighting came from candles, which were made by dipping cloth wicks into hot fat.

Wills, containing lists of household goods, tell us that there was not much furniture, even in wealthy peoples' homes. Their rooms contained furniture made of oak, including tables, stools and chests in which the family kept linen and clothing. Four-poster beds are often mentioned in wills. They had no springs and the feather mattresses rested on a rope framework.

The list below is part of the will of a wealthy Sussex knight. There were no spelling rules, but it is fairly easy to understand if you say the words aloud. Write out the list in present-day spelling and then opposite it, make a list of the items in your own kitchen at home.

In the Kytchine

Item – one boyler for beefe, 7 spitts, 2 brasse potts, one fryinge panne, one greate paire of iron racks, 3 pott hangers, 2 gredirons, one brasse kettell, a bread grater, a spice morter, a chopping kniffe, one furnesse to boyle beefe in, 3 pair of pott hoocks, one iron peele *(used for putting bread in the oven)*, and a great barre of iron before the ffyre.

In the 2nd Bedcamber

Item – 2 borded bedsteeds, one flocke bedd, one fether boulster, one blancquette and one old coverlett.

Long houses

In the highland regions of Britain, from Devon to Scotland, where the soils are poor and farming is difficult, the farmer's home was a simple stone house. It is called a long house because of its shape, which was long and low, usually with only one storey. The farmers earned their living by keeping cattle for their milk, and in its simplest form the long house was home for both the family and its animals. One end of the house had living-quarters and a dairy, where butter and cheese were made. At the other end, through a passage-

A long house which has been restored and turned into a museum on the island of Lewis, Scotland.

way, there was the 'byre' (cattle stalls), or 'shippen' as it was called in Devon.

In Scotland, the divisions of the long house were called the 'ben' (the animals' end) and the 'but' (the living end). The 'but' was the living-room, kitchen and bedroom, with box beds along one wall. In time, these long houses had additional rooms built on them. Sometimes a bedroom was made under the roof and an upper storey was added. The byre was often separated from the living-quarters and had its own outside door.

Until the nineteenth century, some houses in the Scottish highlands and islands had a fireplace in the centre of the living-room, with the smoke finding its way out through the roof. These homes were called 'black houses', because the smoke from the fire turned the ceiling black.

Look for long houses when you visit Devon, Wales or Scotland. They are still used as farms. Copy the sketch below and add the following captions: entrance to house, entrance to byre, bedroom, living-room, dairy, thatch roof, local building stone, store above byre.

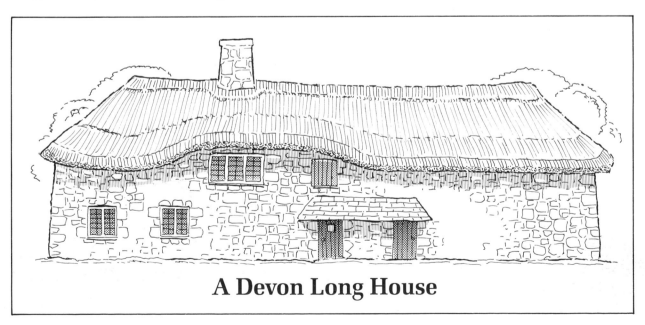

A Devon Long House

A farmhouse in the 1700s

Many farmers lived in farmhouses with large rooms and elaborate furnishings, quite unlike the small cottages of the farm workers they employed. Farmhouses were built of local stone or brick. They had a central front door, with windows on either side. The front door opened into a large hall with a wide staircase leading to the rooms above. The main rooms in the house were the parlour, the dining-room and the kitchen.

The kitchen and hall had floors of earth, brick or stone, whereas the parlour, dining-room and bedrooms had wooden floors. A wealthy farmer had his walls covered with wallpaper, which was then very fashionable, but in most houses the plastered walls were white-washed. If he could afford it, the farmer had furniture made from mahogany, a dark wood brought over from the West Indies.

Although the main rooms might be attractively furnished, there was no proper water supply. Water came from a pump or drained off the roof into lead water cisterns. For sewage, there was an outside lavatory built over a pit. Servants and farm hands slept in rooms under the roof. A dairy farmer needed maids to milk and make cheese, while a farmer growing crops employed ploughboys. At the back of the farmhouse, there was usually a brew-house, a dairy and also a bake-house.

Make a sketch of the farmhouse in the photograph opposite and add labels for: front door, sash windows, servants' bedrooms, chimneys, tablet showing date built.

Opposite *Here is a beautifully kept example of an eighteenth-century farmhouse in southern England.*

Stately homes

Have you ever visited a stately home? Very wealthy people could afford to have magnificent homes to live in, where they could show off their paintings and furniture. Hopetoun House, near Edinburgh, was built in 1699 for the first Earl of Hopetoun. The house was later enlarged on a very grand scale.

In some stately homes, like Hopetoun House, there are hundreds of rooms, but only a few are open to the public. These are usually the elaborately decorated main rooms, such as the library, drawing-rooms, bedrooms, gallery and kitchens. Some of these rooms may have been built as 'state apartments', as they were at Blenheim Palace, in Oxfordshire, and only used on very special occasions. Very few guided tours take you through the servants' quarters, where fifty or more servants lived. When you visit one of these homes, remember that they were once lit with candles and not by electricity.

In the finest of the stately homes, the water supply was well organized. At Chatsworth, built in 1696 for the Duke of Devonshire, cisterns collected spring water from the moors and lead pipes

---

Name of stately home _____

Date of visit _____

1 When was the house built? _____

2 Who was it built for? _____

3 What was the main building material used?_____

4 How many rooms are there? _____

5 What are the names of the most important rooms?_____

_____

_____

6 Make a sketch of an item in the house that interests you.

*One of the state
apartments of Blenheim
palace, in Oxfordshire.*

took it to different parts of the house. There were
flushing lavatories and baths with hot and cold
water. At Wimpole Hall, in Cambridgeshire, a
special bath-house was built with water heated
from below.

Because lavatories in large houses were few
and far between, commodes, (chairs or cabinets
containing chamber-pots) were placed in bedrooms and other rooms.

Make a list of questions to use when you next
visit a stately home. The chart opposite will give
you some ideas for it.

5 | The Middle Ages

The manor house

In the Middle Ages, the manor house was the largest and finest home in the village. The lord of the manor owned much of the local land and the villagers worked on his farm. Some manor houses were fortified and surrounded by a moat, just like the nobles' castles.

The main room of the manor was the hall. The floor was of beaten earth or stone slabs and covered with straw or reeds. The walls were sometimes decorated with brightly coloured paintings or beautiful tapestries. Windows were small because glass was very expensive. At the beginning of the Middle Ages, all warmth was

The 'Great Hall' of Penshurst Place in Kent.

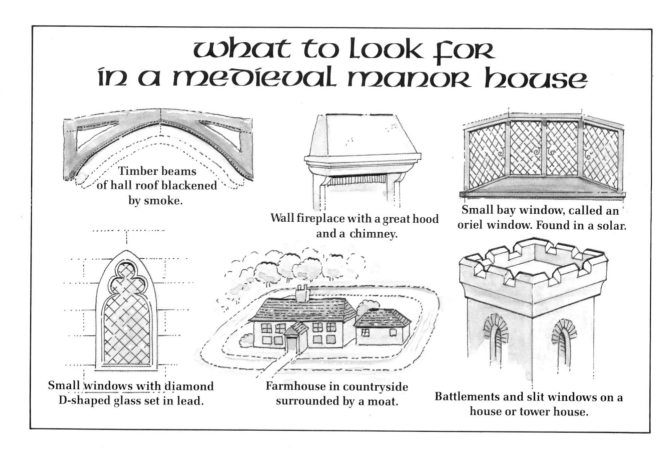

What to Look For in a Medieval Manor House

Timber beams of hall roof blackened by smoke.

Wall fireplace with a great hood and a chimney.

Small bay window, called an oriel window. Found in a solar.

Small windows with diamond D-shaped glass set in lead.

Farmhouse in countryside surrounded by a moat.

Battlements and slit windows on a house or tower house.

provided by a wood fire in the middle of the hall. Its smoke drifted out through the windows or the roof. Later, fireplaces were made against an outside wall and chimneys were built.

Leading off the hall were a kitchen, pantry and buttery, where drink was kept. On the floor above were bedrooms and a small sitting-room, called a 'solar' because it was usually built on the sunny side of the house. There was little furniture and family possessions were kept in a large oak chest. Beds were wooden frames covered by planks, on which a straw mattress was placed.

In Scotland, a laird (lord) might live in a tower house built of stone. For protection, living-rooms were on the first and second floors, which were reached by narrow, winding stairs.

Use the chart above to hunt for clues in an old manor house near you.

The homes of country people

In contrast with the manor house, the villagers lived in huts which were poorly made and provided little more than a shelter from the weather. In the thirteenth century, people began to build cottages with a simple timber frame. This frame was made of crucks, large curved beams which supported both the roof and the side walls of the

A section of the Bayeux tapestry which shows the houses of country people in the eleventh century.

cottage. The walls were made of woven branches (wattle) and overed with mud mixed with straw (daub). The roof was thatched with reeds or straw.

The house consisted of one room, with an earth floor covered with rushes. There are accounts of rushes being very dirty and coated with chicken and pig droppings. Smoke from a fire in the middle of the room made its way out through a hole in the roof or small window openings in the walls. The furniture was never more than a few stools and a board on trestles as a table. People slept fully clothed on heather and straw. A tax record for 1301 lists the possessions of Alice Reyner, a poor villager, as: *1 poor robe, 1 brass posnet* (large pot) *and 1 tripod* (to stand over the open fire), *3 bushels* (1 bushel = 36 litres) *of barley, 6 bushels of oatmeal, a pig, tubs and troughs.*

In time, some village people prospered and built larger homes with two rooms, the additional room being for their animals. The homes of village people have not survived, but cottages made later, using crucks, can still be seen.

Make a list of the main items of your personal property. Compare it with a friend's list.

This diagram shows how a cruck house was constructed during the Middle Ages.

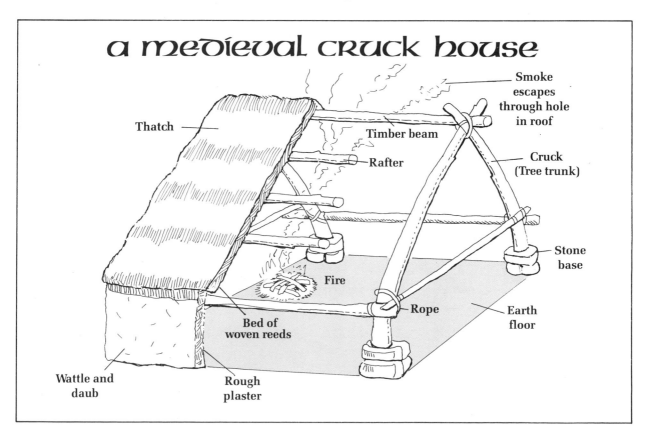

a medieval cruck house

- Thatch
- Timber beam
- Rafter
- Smoke escapes through hole in roof
- Cruck (Tree trunk)
- Stone base
- Fire
- Rope
- Earth floor
- Bed of woven reeds
- Wattle and daub
- Rough plaster

6 Saxon homes

There are no Saxon homes to be seen in Britain today, but thanks to a sandstorm about 700 years ago, the traces of one village have been preserved. At West Stow in Suffolk, a Saxon village built before AD 650 has been excavated and partly rebuilt, using the same materials and methods as the original builders.

The Saxons settled in Britain during the fourth and fifth centuries AD, and remains of their way of life show that they were skilled carpenters and craftsmen and hard-working farmers. Their houses were built over a hollow, which acted as a damp course, keeping the oak floors dry. The

Saxon villagers busily building a new house. Many of our towns and villages have been built in places where Saxon villages once stood.

A view of some of the rebuilt Saxon houses at West Stow, in Suffolk.

walls were of carefully joined, split oak logs and the thatched roofs were supported on woven hazel branches. There was no chimney, but an earth hearth near the doorway was used as a fire place and for cooking. All the family's activities took place in the one room of the house, which may have had a partition at one end.

Around the house were other buildings: a small granary for the barley, and workshops which could be used for spinning and weaving wool, grinding corn or forging iron.

Other Saxon village sites include the ones at Catholme, near Burton-upon-Trent, and at Charlton in Hampshire.

Imagine you were a young Saxon living at West Stow. Write a description of an evening in your home. Design a poster to attract people to visit the West Stow Saxon village.

7 A Roman villa

Wealthy landowners in Roman Britain built homes with all the comforts and decorations of similar houses in Italy. The buildings which made up a farm were called a villa, and their remains can be found in parts of southern England. Villas were designed with a courtyard edged by blocks of rooms, forming wings. Chedworth in Gloucestershire is an example of one of the more luxurious villas.

The north wing included a row of bedrooms, a bath suite with 'hot' rooms at different temperatures, and a pool for a cold plunge. In the west wing there were more baths, with rooms heated by steam. They were reached along a corridor

Some of the mosaics found by archaeologists at the Fishbourne Roman palace.

Part of the hypocaust heating system discovered at the Roman palace in Fishbourne, West Sussex.

from a row of bedrooms. On the same corridor, there was a magnificent dining-room with a heated, mosaic floor.

The kitchen was close by in the south wing, together with servants' rooms and a lavatory. The seating in the lavatory was set over a sewer and in front of the seats piped water flowed into a wash-basin. This water was used to rinse the sponges on sticks, which took the place of toilet paper in the Roman world.

Many rooms in the villa had decorations which matched those in fashionable Italian villas. Statues of gods and goddesses made the rooms even more attractive.

Imagine you are a Roman estate agent selling a villa. Write an advertisement to attract buyers. Illustrate your advertisement with a view of part of the villa.

what to look for at a roman villa

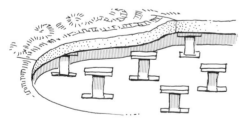

Under-floor heating. Hollow under floor to take hot air from furnace. Floor supported on pillars. This is called hypocaust heating.

Mosaic floors. Tiny squares of stone and pottery laid on a cement base. The work of unskilled apprentices is less neat and mistakes may be spotted.

Sculptures and carvings. Sometimes carvings appear as reliefs: they are carved in the top layers of a stone block.

Box tile flue to carry off smoke and fumes from heating system and heat the walls. They were cemented end to end.

Stoke holes for furnaces, once fired with wood or charcoal. Hot air flowed through channels in floors and walls.

8 Iron Age homes

About 700 BC, the first of the Celts arrived from western Europe to farm the land in Britain. These people knew how to make iron tools, so this period is called the Iron Age. Archaeologists have studied the sites where the Celts lived and the clues they have found give us a good idea of how the people built their homes and what they were like to live in.

Using the evidence from an Iron Age farm site in Dorset, a house has been built in the Queen Elizabeth Country Park near Petersfield, Hampshire. The house is circular with an upright centre pole, to which other wooden poles were attached to make a framework. The low walls were made of wattle and daub (see page 30) and the roof was thatched. Four tonnes of thatch were needed for the roof and the timber came from more than 200 young trees. Inside there was an earth hearth where food could be cooked in clay ovens or over the wood fire.

A rebuilt Iron Age house in the Queen Elizabeth Country Park in Hampshire.

make a model of an iron age house

You will need:
30cm² piece of chipboard.
90cm of 6mm (¼″) dowelling.
Modelling clay or Blutack.
Art straws.
Wood glue.
Card 12cm x 30cm.
Paint.

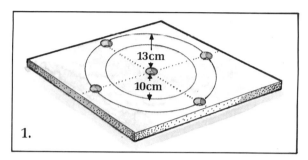

1.

1. Mark the centre of the chipboard. Mark with a compass two circles 10cm and 13cm from the centre. Get an adult to drill a hole about 5cm deep with a 6mm (¼″) drill bit. Mark 4 positions on the 13cm circle, as shown. Drill 4 holes with ¼″ drill bit at an angle pointing to a spot about 14cm above the centre hole.

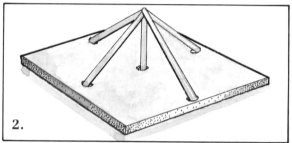

2.

2. Cut dowelling with centre pole length of 14cm; other poles length 19cm. Glue dowelling into holes and glue at centre or secure with fine wire.

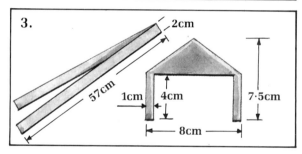

3.

3. Cut a strip of card 57cm long and 2cm wide. (You will have to join two pieces together to get the correct length.) Cut the doorway in a piece of card as shown.

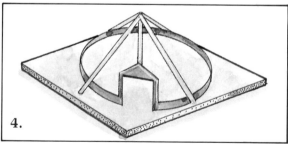

4.

4. Secure the strip of card upright along the 10cm diameter line with modelling clay. It should just touch the inside edge of the 4 poles. Glue or staple the doorway to the ends of the card.

5. Cut lengths of art straws 15cm long and glue to edge of card and top of hut. Add extra pieces around side of doorway to cover hut completely. Colour art straws and wall.

You have made an Iron Age hut in a similar way to the methods used by Iron Age people.

5.

9 The first homes

Nearly 4,000 years ago, during the New Stone Age, the homes of people living at Skara Brae, on the Orkney Islands, were buried by sandstorms. The area has been excavated and seven huts have been found. They were built of stone, because wood is very scarce on the islands. The huts are shaped like squares. Because Skara Brae gets very strong winds and storms, the huts were buried under earth and peat after they were built, leaving only a hole in the roof to let out the smoke.

The roofs have long since fallen in, but because all the furniture was made of stone, which does not rot, we have a very good idea of what the

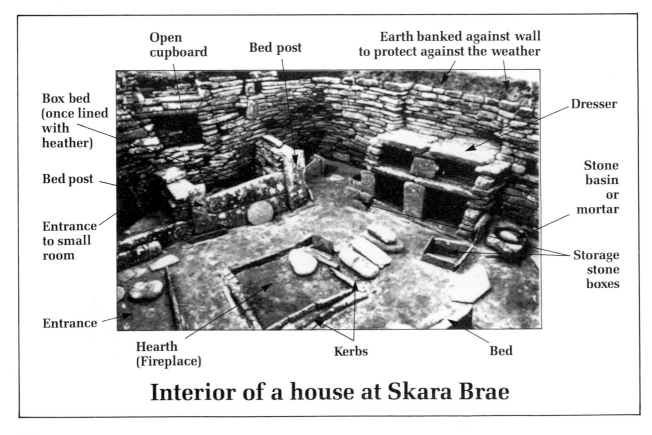

Interior of a house at Skara Brae

Labels: Open cupboard · Bed post · Earth banked against wall to protect against the weather · Box bed (once lined with heather) · Dresser · Bed post · Stone basin or mortar · Entrance to small room · Storage stone boxes · Entrance · Hearth (Fireplace) · Kerbs · Bed

homes were like. They had beds lined with heather, stone storage boxes and even a stone dresser against one wall. A small room at the side was probably used as a lavatory, since it contains a stone drain. Narrow tunnels from the houses, roofed with stone, led out to a paved area in the open air.

Many thousands of years ago, caves were used as homes as they offered shelter from the weather and protection from wild animals. The people who lived in them were nomadic hunters and food-gatherers and did not stay long in any one place. Relics left in caves — for example, at Cheddar in Somerset, Creswell in Derbyshire, and Kent's Cavern near Torquay — prove that caves were used. Relics have also been found in Lincolnshire, which show that these ancient people also had homes in the open. The relics can be seen in the British Museum, in London, and in museums near the sites.

Imagine you are living at Skara Brae, 4,000 years ago. Describe a typical day in your life.

The homes at Skara Brae were buried beneath earth and peat to shelter them from strong winds and storms.

10 Projects on homes

Exploring a house

Exploring old homes in your neighbourhood can be great fun if you go about it the right way. Just looking at the outside of an old house will tell you something about the way it was built, but very little about what the rooms are like and what it was like to live there in the past.

If you decide to do a project on a house, then you must choose one that you can visit. It need not be a timber-framed Tudor home, a nineteenth-century terrace house can be just as interesting and still contain many clues about life in it when it was new. Perhaps you have a relation or friend who lives in an old house and will let you look over it. Stately homes and many of the large houses open to the public are too large and too well described in guidebooks to make an interesting study. Having found a suitable house, use the chart opposite to help you plan your research.

Perhaps you would prefer to explore one aspect of homes in the past rather than a particular home. Here are some ideas for projects:

the kitchen and its equipment
lighting the home
glass in the home
keeping warm indoors
bedrooms and their furniture
lavatories and bathrooms

Some advice: do not choose a topic such as 'furniture', which is too large for you to finish in the time available.

Opposite *Here are suggestions for organizing your project on an old house.*

You will often find old household gadgets and equipment on stalls in a local street market.

ORGANIZING A PROJECT ON AN OLD HOUSE

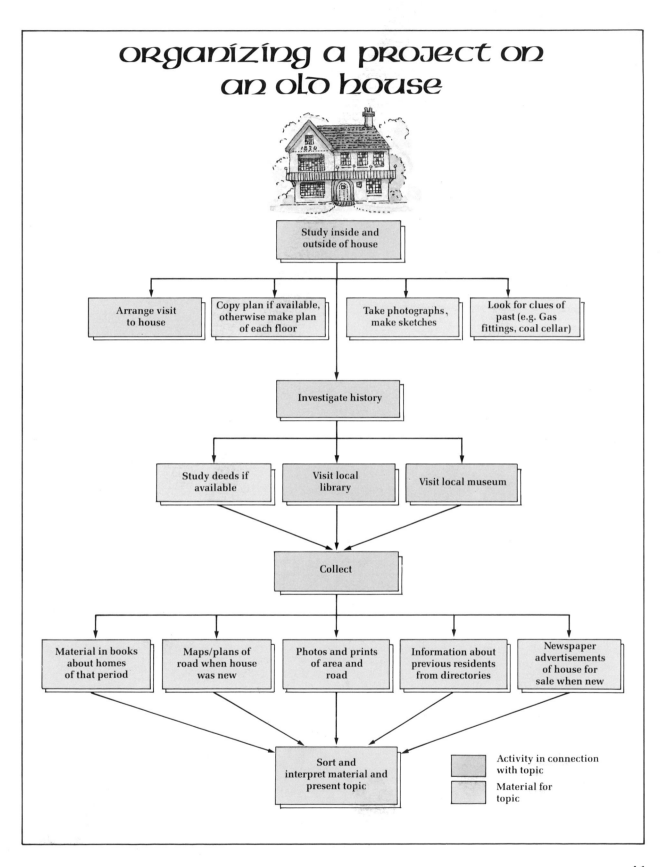

Study inside and outside of house

- **Arrange visit to house**
- **Copy plan if available, otherwise make plan of each floor**
- **Take photographs, make sketches**
- **Look for clues of past (e.g. Gas fittings, coal cellar)**

Investigate history

- **Study deeds if available**
- **Visit local library**
- **Visit local museum**

Collect

- **Material in books about homes of that period**
- **Maps/plans of road when house was new**
- **Photos and prints of area and road**
- **Information about previous residents from directories**
- **Newspaper advertisements of house for sale when new**

Sort and interpret material and present topic

Legend:
- Activity in connection with topic
- Material for topic

Looking at one aspect of the home

Instead of studying a house, you may prefer to explore one aspect of homes, such as how they have been heated, or how kitchens and their equipment have changed. Here are some information sources for this type of project.

What older people can tell you

Ask your parents and grandparents what kitchens were like when they were young. They may know where you can see old-fashioned appliances, such as a wooden mangle or a flat iron.

Second-hand shops, stalls and less-expensive antique shops

Some household gadgets and equipment can be found on market stalls and in second-hand shops. Look out for such things as warming-pans and coal tongs.

Old catalogues, magazines and books

The reference section of your local library or a second-hand bookshop may have old illustrated catalogues which firms, such as the Army and

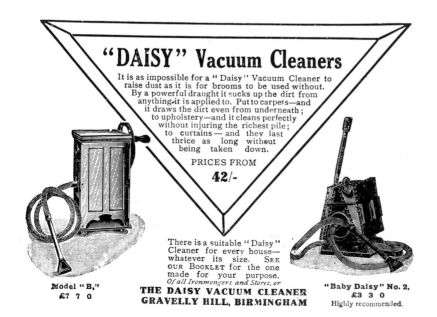

Old magazines and catalogues will contain advertisements, like this one, for household equipment. Can you work out what the price of these vacuum cleaners would be today?

A nineteenth-century terraced house, like one of these, can be just as interesting for a project as a building that is hundreds of years old.

Navy Stores, used to print. Old magazines may contain advertisements for furniture, cookers and similar household goods. Books on home management, such as Mrs Beeton's *Book of Household Management* (first published in 1861), contain descriptions of housework and how to manage servants.

Museums and houses open to the public
Museums may display rooms as they appeared in the past and have exhibitions of items used in the home. Houses open to the public may also have household equipment on display.

Local records
In the reference section of your library or the County Record Office, there may be volumes of the County Archaeological Society's reports. These may include details of wills and descriptions of old houses in the county.

Presenting the project
Make your project attractive to look at and interesting to read. Include lots of illustrations and explain everything in your own words – do not copy from books. A loose-leaf file with a section for each chapter is a simple and practical way of showing your work.

11 Homes in the future

People in 1939 would never have believed that in fifty year's time many families would take their meals out of a freezer, heat them in a microwave oven and sit down to eat them a few minutes later. What will homes be like in another fifty year's time? Will all meals be prepared automatically at the press of a button? How will homes be heated?

Discuss with your friends what your homes may look like in the year 2040. Draw sketches of the rooms and their furnishings. Under your sketches, give reasons for the choices you have made. Describe the shapes and materials used for the furniture and other items.

This is a very up-to-date kitchen. Can you imagine what an up-to-date kitchen will look like in fifty year's time?

Places to visit

Many museums have exhibitions of household equipment and some have rooms set out as they would have looked in houses in the past. Here is a selection of places which will interest you.

Houses open to the public
Avon: The Georgian House, Bristol (18th century)
Ayrshire: Robert Burn's cottage, Alloway (18th century)
Bedfordshire: Woburn Abbey (18th century)
Dorset: Thomas Hardy's cottage, Bockhampton (19th century)
East Sussex: The Clergy House, Alfriston (14th century)
Edinburgh: The Georgian House (18th century) and Gladstone's Land (17th century)
Glasgow: The Tenement House (19th/20th centuries)
Gwynedd: Penrhyn Castle, Caernarfon (19th century)
Isle of Lewis: Arnol (19th-century black house)
Lothian: Borthwick Castle (15th century)
Norfolk: Blickling Hall (17th century)
Shropshire: Stokesay Castle (14th century)
Warwickshire: Anne Hathaway's cottage, Shottery (16th century)
West Sussex: Parham House (16th century)

Museums and country parks
Argyll: Auchendrain (18th/19th-century highland town)
Durham: North of England Open Air Museum, Beamish (19th-century houses)
Edinburgh: Palace of Holyroodhouse (period furniture)
Glamis: Angus Folk Museum (country life)
Gloucestershire: Cirencester Museum (Roman kitchen)
Hampshire: Queen Elizabeth Country Park, Petersfield (Iron Age home)

London: Geffrye Museum (period rooms and furniture) and the Museum of London (relics from houses)

South Glamorgan: Welsh Folk Museum, St Fagan's (old farmhouses and furniture)

Suffolk: West Stow (Saxon homes)

West Sussex: West Dean Open Air Museum, near Chichester (medieval houses)

West Yorkshire: Jorvik Viking Centre, York (10th-century village)

Worcestershire: Avoncroft Museum of Buildings, near Bromsgrove (Iron Age home)

Roman villas
Avon: Gatcombe and King's Weston
Gloucestershire: Chedworth and Great Witcombe
Isle of Wight: Brading
Kent: Lullingstone
Oxfordshire: North Leigh
West Sussex: Bignor
Wiltshire: Littlecote

Further reading

Allen, A., *The Story of Your Home* (Faber and Faber, 1972)
Branigan, K., *Roman Britain* (Readers Digest, 1980)
Crawford, S., *A Family in the Thirties* (Wayland, 1988)
de Haan, D., *Antique Household Gadgets and Appliances* (Blandford, 1977)
Harrison, M., *Homes in History* (Wayland, 1983)
Harrison, M., *Homes in Britain* (Allen and Unwin, 1975)
Harrison, M., *Homes* (Benn, 1973)
Potter, M. and A., *Houses* (Murray, 1973)
Ross, S., *An Edwardian Household* (Wayland, 1986)
Rowland-Entwistle, T., *Houses and Homes* (Wayland, 1985)
Watson, L., *A Celtic Family* (Wayland, 1987)

Glossary

Ben and but   Scottish terms for the living end and the animals' end of a long house.

Black house   A simple house in the highlands and islands of Scotland which had a hearth in the centre of the room.

Box bed   A bed built into one end of a room, which could be hidden behind doors or a curtain.

Buttery   The room in which drink was stored.

Byre   A house or barn used for feeding and sheltering cattle.

Cistern   A tank used for storing water.

Commode   A cabinet or chair which held a chamber-pot.

Copper   A large wash-basin made out of copper, under which there was a fire which could be used to heat up water.

Hearth   The part of the floor on which a fire is made.

Industrial Revolution   The period after about 1760 in which steam power was developed and different types of machines invented, which resulted in Britain becoming the leading industrial country in the world.

Iron Age   The period from about the seventh century BC until the coming of the Romans in 55 BC.

Middle Ages   The period from about AD 1066 to 1500.

Mosaic   A design or picture made up of small pieces of coloured glass, marble or other stones.

New Stone Age   The period from about 4000 to 1800 BC when farmers using stone tools lived in Britain.

Privy   A simple form of lavatory without running water.

Toll-house   The cottage built beside a tollgate, where a fee had to be paid for the use of the road.

Turnpike road   A road built by a private company. Money to pay for it and its maintenance was raised by charging travellers a toll.

Range   An old-fashioned cooker, usually heated by coal. It had an oven and a flat, iron top, often with holes for saucepans.

Scullery   A room off the kitchen for washing-up dishes and doing the laundry.

Wattle and daub   Woven strips of wood covered with clay to form a wall.

Index

Picture Acknowledgements
The publishers would like to thank the following for supplying pictures: Paul Seheult/Chapel Studio Picture Library 6, 7, 20, 43; David Cumming 4, 40; Mary Evans Picture Library 8, 13, 16, 18, 30; Cliff Lines 25, 33, 36; Macdonald/Aldus 9, 12, 39; Mansell 19, 42; TOPHAM 22, 27, 34 (both), 44. The picture on page 17 is from the Wayland Picture Library. All the artwork is by Stephen Wheele, except for the picture by Mark Bergin on page 32.